IMAGES
of America

ROCK ISLAND ARSENAL

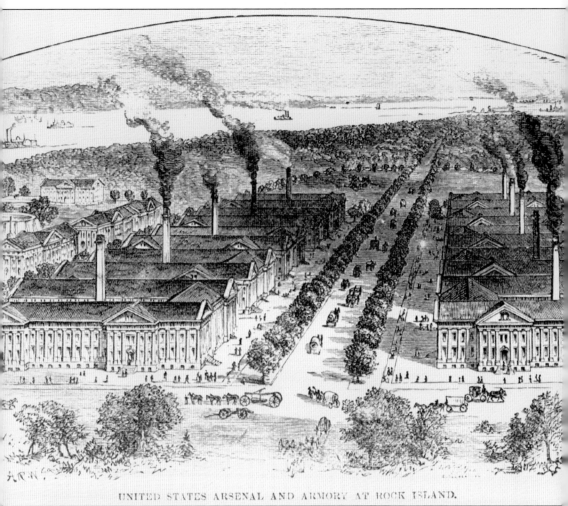

UNITED STATES ARSENAL AND ARMORY AT ROCK ISLAND.

Often, an artist's imagination exceeds the reality on the ground. This sketch from the late 1870s illustrates that point. The 10 manufacturing buildings that are the core of Arsenal Island are shown, but only two tall chimneys and two of the support buildings seen behind the main manufacturing shops were ever built. However, the sketch gives the impression of vitality and action, which was probably the intent. (Courtesy of the Rock Island Arsenal Museum.)

ON THE COVER: Rock Island Arsenal manufactured artillery before the end of the 19th century. The arsenal performed so well during the Spanish-American War (1898–1900) that it was made the national artillery assembly center and designed carriages and caissons. In this 1904 scene, three-inch guns are assembled in Shop G, Building No. 108. The straps ran the machinery. (Courtesy of the Rock Island Arsenal Museum.)

IMAGES
of America

ROCK ISLAND
ARSENAL

George Eaton

ARCADIA
PUBLISHING

Published by Arcadia Publishing
Charleston, South Carolina

Printed in the United States of America

Library of Congress Control Number: 2014936331

For all general information, please contact Arcadia Publishing:
Telephone 843-853-2070
Fax 843-853-0044
E-mail sales@arcadiapublishing.com
For customer service and orders:
Toll-Free 1-888-313-2665

Visit us on the Internet at www.arcadiapublishing.com

This book is dedicated to the historians and museum curators who tell the story of the Rock Island Arsenal and the people who make it run.

CONTENTS

ACKNOWLEDGMENTS

Rock Island Arsenal rose from the hard stone of Rock Island beginning in 1862; however, in reality, Arsenal Island has been the heart of the Quad Cities Area for almost 200 years. As the oldest establishment in the area, the Army's presence on the island affected the towns of Davenport and Bettendorf in Iowa, and Moline and Rock Island in Illinois, as well as numerous other smaller towns in the area. Rock Island Arsenal impacted the area as an employer, business opportunity, and visual cue. The massive stone structures on the island in the middle of the Mississippi River stand out and draw attention. One still notices the energy and activity of the Army's last great arsenal able to melt, pour, and finish metal; receive, store, and issue materiel; run a 130-year-old bridge; and, more quietly, manage a massive proportion of the Army's logistics infrastructure.

Of great luck in developing this book is the fact that the Army was always interested in documenting its presence on the island. For this volume, I needed to look no further than the collections of the Rock Island Arsenal Museum, the US Army Corps of Engineers Rock Island District Library, and the US Army Sustainment Command History Office Archives for photographs and maps. Publication of this book shines much-deserved light on their efforts to ensure the story of the island is not forgotten.

I would like to especially acknowledge and thank Kris Leinicke, director of the Rock Island Arsenal Museum, along with Jodie Wesemann and Bill Johnson, for all their assistance; Robert Romic of the Corps of Engineers Library; and Kiri Hamilton, a dedicated volunteer at the Army Sustainment Command History Office. In addition, I want to acknowledge Dale Heiser of the museum for assisting in the scanning of photographs. Clyde Cocke and Chris Crawford started this project and passed it to me. Thanks to them for the initial work and the collection of many photographs. Thanks also to Julia Simpson at Arcadia, who kept me on schedule and provided the best advice. Finally, I want to thank the Rock Island Arsenal Historical Society for supporting the Rock Island Arsenal Museum. All of the author's proceeds from this book will be donated to the historical society.

Unless otherwise noted, all photographs are courtesy of the Rock Island Arsenal Museum.

INTRODUCTION

In 1805, Lt. Zebulon Pike set foot on what may have been called Rock Island but is now most often called Arsenal Island. The future home of Rock Island Arsenal was uninhabited, but it was known as a summer retreat for the local Sauk and Meskwaki tribes. In his autobiography, Black Hawk described the island:

> It was our garden, like the white people have near their big villages, which supplied us with strawberries, blackberries, gooseberries, plums, apples and nuts of different kinds. Being situated at the foot of the rapids, its waters supplied us with the finest fish. In my early life I spent many happy days on this island. A good spirit had charge of it, which lived in a cave in the rocks immediately under the place where the fort now stands. This guardian spirit has often been seen by our people. It was white, with large wings like a swan's, but ten times larger.

To the Army, the island was more important as a potential spot to provide security along the Mississippi River. While the Unites States had, through the Louisiana Purchase, just acquired the west bank of the river and hundreds of thousands of square miles, even the east bank of the Mississippi north of St. Louis was beyond the frontier and unknown territory. Pike's explorations were intended to find the headwaters of the Mississippi, which he missed, and develop information and maps about the river and its inhabitants, at which he was more successful. Rock Island was, and remains, the largest island on the Mississippi at over 900 acres. Located at the end of the dangerous Rock Island Rapids, the island presented an opportunity to control the upper Mississippi River by regulating traffic at the rapids. This concept of traffic control increased over time, as larger boats and then steamboats plied the waters.

In addition to the rapids, the island allowed the Army to keep an eye on the local Native American tribes who were disgruntled with the United States over the terms of the Sauk and Fox Treaty of 1804, which had transferred over 52 million acres of land to the Americans. Unhappy with the treaty when Pike arrived, the frustration led some of the tribe to ally with the British in the War of 1812. These warriors, eventually known as the "British Band" of the Sauk and Fox, under the leadership of Black Hawk, fought and defeated the Americans in the area at Campbells Island and Credit Island in the summer of 1814. These defeats led to the establishment of Fort Armstrong on Rock Island in May 1816. The fort was the first permanent settlement in the area, providing security for fur traders, river transportation, and, after the mid-1820s, settlers. Fort Armstrong was the administrative and logistics hub for the field forces during the Black Hawk War of 1832. After that war, with the frontier moving farther west, the fort was abandoned. At times under the control of a caretaker and at other times used as a supply depot, the old fort faded away.

One of the caretakers was George Davenport, considered the first permanent settler in the area. Davenport had been in the Army during the War of 1812 and then became a sutler—a contractor who provided food and other supplies to Army units. Eventually, he quit that role and became a fur trader and land developer, building a large trading post and a modern home on the island. In 1845, just weeks before he was murdered, Davenport hosted a meeting in his house with railroad interests and discussed the possibility of erecting a rail bridge over the Mississippi at Rock Island. Based on the engineering capacity of the day, Rock Island was the only place a bridge could be placed and still be far enough south to be financially effective. Bridges could cross from the Illinois mainland to the island and then jump the main river channel to Davenport. The shallowness of the rapids and the shorter spans made this a perfect spot. While Illinois and Iowa soon granted licenses to the Chicago–Rock Island line and the Mississippi and Missouri lines, the federal government refused to grant a license to cross the island. Jefferson Davis was the secretary of war and was working for a rail crossing much farther south that would potentially allow the spread of slaveholding states across the southern tier. Eventually, the rail companies took advantage of the Act of 1852, which allowed rails to cross public lands, and proceeded to build across the island. Davis tried again to block construction but was overruled by the Supreme Court. In March 1856, the first bridge over the Mississippi River opened and the area became the transportation hub of the United States. Only two weeks after the bridge opened, the steamer *Effie Afton* ran into the structure (probably on purpose) and, after getting all the cargo and passengers off, burst into flames. Lawsuits ensued, with the Supreme Court eventually dealing a blow to the water transport industry by ruling that bridges could be built over any American waterway, but that ships would be granted the right-of-way. That same bridge was rebuilt several times over the next 15 years.

In the late 1850s, the Army was desirous of building a storage and maintenance depot to service the Army on the western frontier. After several scouting operations, the rail and water transportation nexus at Rock Island—along with the potential for waterpower using the slough between the island and the Illinois mainland—made Rock Island the obvious choice for a new arsenal. On July 11, 1862, President Lincoln signed legislation creating the Rock Island Arsenal. Maj. Charles Kingsbury arrived in 1863 as the first Rock Island Arsenal commander. He was provided a plan to build three structures on the west end of the island, essentially on top of the Fort Armstrong site. In 1864, he began construction of what is now called the Clocktower Building, the only one of the three planned structures that was built. Kingsbury also began efforts to create waterpower. Neither of these efforts were complete by the time Kingsbury left the Arsenal in 1865.

Kingsbury had competition on the island for labor and materials in the form of the Rock Island Prison Barracks, a prisoner-of-war camp for Confederate prisoners. Construction of the camp, designed to hold 10,000 prisoners, began in August 1863. Over 12,500 Confederates came through the camp between December 1863 and June 1865. Almost 2,000 prisoners died, primarily from infectious disease. A significant number of prisoners also chose to enlist in the Union army in order to escape prison life, while about 40 successfully escaped. Nothing remains from the camp other than the Confederate Cemetery and burial plots for guards in the Federal Cemetery.

After the Civil War ended, Brig. Gen. Thomas Rodman was assigned to Rock Island Arsenal with a new plan for the future. Rather than a storage and maintenance facility, the Army needed Rock Island Arsenal as a manufacturing center to replace facilities lost in the Civil War and to establish an arsenal in the middle of the country to support both coasts and the frontier. Rodman finished the Clocktower Building in 1867 and, at the same time, designed a massive manufacturing center in the middle of the island. Under Rodman's plan, the new arsenal consisted of 10 main shop buildings, support buildings, a reservoir, and waterpower dams. He soon pushed to relocate the original bridge to the west end of the island, farther away from manufacturing operations. That bridge was completed in 1872, about a year after Rodman's death in June 1871. Although still a debated point, this author believes Rodman died in the commanding officer's quarters he designed and began building in 1869. Capt. Daniel Flagler took over and continued the construction process, primarily completing Rodman's plan while making some adjustments. Construction of the shop buildings lasted until 1893. During this time the dam was also built, along with several other sets of officer quarters.

This period was not just a time of construction. As soon as the Civil War was over, excess ammunition and Army material were sent to Rock Island Arsenal for storage, maintenance, and overhaul. Eventually, much of the ammunition was recycled for its brass and iron components. Artillery pieces were stored in huge gun parks. As soon as possible, the arsenal began manufacturing items for the Army and began to supply material to units on the frontier. In 1896, as a culmination of construction, a new Government Bridge was finished. That bridge is still used today.

In 1898, the Spanish-American War broke out, and, for the first time, the Rock Island Arsenal supported a war effort overseas. By this time, the arsenal made every kind of equipment a soldier needed except for small arms. Fork and mess kit, haversack and ammunition belts, saddle and reins, artillery and caissons—all were manufactured at Rock Island. By 1898, the arsenal was known for making artillery, except the gun tube itself, which was manufactured at another site. Rock Island Arsenal made a name for itself from 1898 to 1902 and was rewarded in 1904 when half of the 1903 Springfield 30.06 Rifle production was directed to Rock Island.

In the years leading up to World War I, the arsenal maintained a steady rate of production with minor modernization. A golf course was begun in 1894, and a 99-year lease to use land on Arsenal Island was granted the Rock Island Arsenal Golf Club in 1904. World War I saw a huge increase in production and employment at Rock Island Arsenal. Almost 15,000 people were working on the arsenal at the height of production, in addition to many construction workers. New, modern artillery was too big for the old stone shops, and a new building was erected. An ammunition plant was built as well, along with myriad other temporary buildings. After the war, dozens of storage buildings and smaller shops were constructed to house excess. The interwar period was one of low employment but continuous experimentation and development. The first American tank was built on the arsenal in 1920, and Rock Island Arsenal became the center of tank development until 1939. Modern artillery was developed and manufactured. Armored cars were developed. Machine guns and rifles were refurbished. The Rock Island Ordnance Depot was created to manage the receipt, storage, and issue of repaired parts. While employment dropped as low as 650 at the depth of the Great Depression, the arsenal continued to provide support to the Army.

In addition to development and manufacturing, the interwar period saw the end of the Rock Island Rapids as an obstacle to free navigation of the Mississippi River. As early as 1837, Lt. Robert E. Lee had been dispatched to Rock Island to map the rapids and determine the navigation channel. The Army Corps of Engineers had blasted out parts of the rapids in an effort to create a minimum four-foot, and then six-foot, depth. The Moline locks and lateral dams in the river had been built in an attempt to bypass the worst of the rapids. The movement of the bridge to its current location also eased navigation by putting the swing span in the middle of the channel. In the early 1930s, Congress decreed that a nine-foot navigation channel was to be created and maintained through the construction of a series of locks and dams north of St. Louis. The very first of these was built at Rock Island Arsenal, tying in to the 1896 Government Bridge. Finally, in 1934, the Rock Island Rapids were erased when the water level rose 20 feet. No longer was Arsenal Island an isolated fortress sitting high above the water.

World War II did not spring unexpectedly on Rock Island Arsenal in December 1941. There had been clear indications that the United States would enter the war, and the arsenal had been ramping up for several years. Rock Island had helped train commercial firms on the manufacture of military items before the war. New machine guns were perfected in 1940. A new method of rifling barrels was perfected in 1941, making mass-production of rifles possible. Artillery was updated. In December 1941, all the arsenal had to do was hire more employees to begin producing on a full scale. The arsenal continued to support the war, employing almost 20,000. More new shops were constructed, as well as modern office buildings. The Rock Island Arsenal was honored many times by the Army for its efforts.

At war's end in 1945, Rock Island Arsenal was at its peak. Since then, no other conflict has required the scope of effort or the number of employees. This does not mean that the arsenal has not continued to support the Army. The Korean War saw a surge of activity, as did the Vietnam War. New artillery and missile launch items were designed and produced, and a test and evaluation center was built. Over time, higher logistics organizations were moved to Rock Island Arsenal and occupied buildings. Finally, in the mid-1980s, a modern foundry and shop was constructed, utilizing the buildings constructed in World War I and World War II and adding a half mile of new facilities. Most of the old stone shops were converted to office space. Today, the Rock Island Arsenal continues to manufacture critical items for the Department of Defense and houses several national-level logistics organizations. The Arsenal remains the largest employer in the area. For over 150 years, Rock Island Arsenal has been the heart of the Quad Cities Area.

One

BEFORE THE ARSENAL

Rock Island Arsenal was created in July 1862. Rock Island had been occupied by the Army on and off since 1816, when Fort Armstrong was built. Fort Armstrong was sited on the island in part to keep an eye on Black Hawk and the "British Band" of the Sauk and Fox tribes. This was the title the Army had given those who had sided with the British in the War of 1812. In addition, the Army wanted to control the upper Mississippi through a fort on the Rock Island Rapids, a notoriously dangerous part of the river. Fort Armstrong performed both tasks. During the Black Hawk War of 1832, Fort Armstrong was the administrative and logistics center for the engaged Army forces. Gen. Winfield Scott eventually established his headquarters there. After the Black Hawk War, treaties were signed that pushed all of the Native Americans in the area west of the Mississippi River. In 1836, Fort Armstrong was temporarily abandoned as the Army moved farther west.

One of the caretakers for Fort Armstrong after 1836 was George Davenport. He is considered the first permanent settler in the area. Eventually, Davenport built a large house on Rock Island. He was a local instigator for building a railroad bridge using Rock Island as a stepping stone over the river at the Rock Island Rapids. The bridge was completed in April 1856, some 11 years after the process started. Overnight, the local area was the transportation hub of the United States, while creating conflict between rail and water transportation interests.

Meanwhile, other local inhabitants and squatters used the island and the waterpower offered by the river to create the beginnings of industry in the area. The most notable of these was David Sears, who built a mill and dam. He also developed plans for a subdivision of Moline, Illinois, to be built on the southeast part of the island. These latter plans came to naught, but Sears had made such improvements that, when the Army retook control of the island in 1862 and forced the squatters off, only Sears and Davenport were compensated.

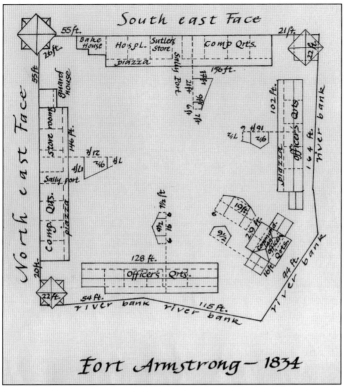

The Army began construction of Fort Armstrong in May 1816. This drawing was produced in 1834 by an unknown Army engineer. It shows the buildings and dimensions of the fort. While an imposing site on the river, each side of the fort was only 300 feet long. The drawing shows that everything needed for the fort was inside the walls, from the barracks to the hospital and sutler store.

Rock Island Arsenal and the local area held a major celebration in 1916 on the centennial of the fort. This scale model was manufactured in 1916 and then donated to the Rock Island Arsenal Museum. The model shows how the fort only had two walls. In 1816, the island stood 20 feet above the water. Those bluffs provided security for the river sides of the fort.

As part of the centennial celebration, local craftsmen built a replica of one of the fort's three blockhouses. This photograph from 1916 shows the blockhouse and the limestone bluffs. In the background, the 1896 bridge is visible. The blockhouse still stands today, nearly 100 years later, as Rock Island Arsenal prepares to celebrate the fort's bicentennial.

A VIEW OF FORT ARMSTRONG, ROCK ISLAND, MISSISSIPPI RIVER.

In 1840, artist D.P. McKown produced this drawing of Fort Armstrong. There may be some errors in the drawing, as there was no fence on the water side of the fort. Although the fort was abandoned in 1836, by 1840, it was being used as a storage depot. Perhaps the new occupants added more walls. The drawing does show the caves Black Hawk mentions in his description of the island.

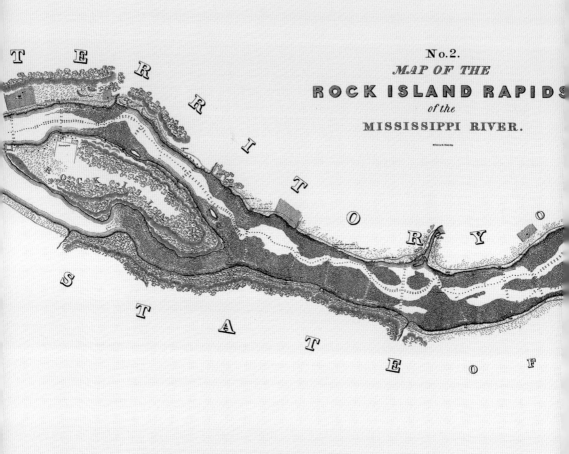

The Rock Island Rapids were a major obstacle to free navigation of the upper Mississippi River. As early as 1833, the US Army Corps of Engineers worked to improve navigation, especially after steamboats began to operate up the river. In 1837, Lt. Robert E. Lee was charged with mapping the Rock Island Rapids. Establishing himself on an abandoned steamboat sunk in the rapids, he carefully mapped the 12-mile length and the many fingers of rock that impinged on the channel.

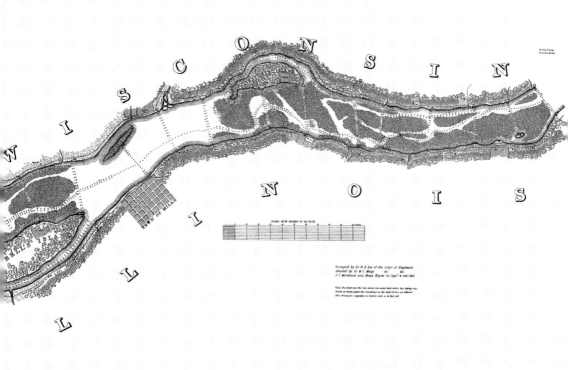

His map shows the winding channel that befuddled most captains. To safely navigate the rapids, boats would pick up a pilot at Rock Island to get them to LeClaire. They would drop off the pilot, who would then wait for a downstream boat in need of his services. (Courtesy of the US Army Corps of Engineers Rock Island Library.)

In 1845, the fort was again abandoned. The weather and a series of fires slowly ate away at the structures. This photograph was taken in the early to mid-1850s. The commander's house and one of the blockhouses are already gone. In 1855 or 1856, a fire, perhaps set by those building the bridge, consumed the rest of the fort. (Courtesy of the US Army Sustainment Command History Office.)

This anonymous drawing shows the rapids. Besides a wandering channel, the rapids were full of small islands and submerged snags. There are several boats in close proximity in the drawing, which would not have been smart navigation. If one got stuck, the others could run into it. The hillside clearing on the left may be where the treaty was signed after the Black Hawk War.

This photograph purportedly shows one of the steamboats that supplied Fort Armstrong during the Black Hawk War of 1832. If so, the boat is below Rock Island and downstream from the end of the rapids. That would be as far upriver as the boat could steam with the side load. (Courtesy of the US Army Sustainment Command History Office.)

This drawing by H. Thompson depicts the treaty ceremony after the Black Hawk War. Seated is the governor of Illinois, with Gen. Winfield Scott behind him. Antoine LeClaire interprets. The identities of the Native Americans are unknown. The treaty removed the Sauk and Meskwaki from Illinois and pushed them far west of the Mississippi.

During the Black Hawk War, the commanding general of the Army, Winfield Scott, was ordered west to supplement the meager forces in the area. He arrived with his force decimated by cholera. He established his headquarters at Fort Armstrong in the commander's quarters. This photograph shows the house before it burned around 1850. (Courtesy of the US Army Sustainment Command History Office.)

The Black Hawk War brought many future notables to the area. Besides Scott, Abraham Lincoln, Jefferson Davis, and Zachary Taylor, seven future US senators and six future governors of Midwest states participated in the conflict. Just like today, veterans held reunions many years later. The seated man third from the left is Gen. Samuel Whiteside of the Illinois militia. (Courtesy of the Hauberg Museum, Black Hawk State Park.)

George Davenport (right) was the first permanent settler in the area. Born in Britain, he moved to the United States and served in the Army in the War of 1812. After the war, he was hired as a sutler to Fort Armstrong, providing food and other supplies. He soon quit that work for the more lucrative fur-trading business and also bought up large amounts of land after 1825. During the Black Hawk War, he worked for the state of Illinois as a quartermaster at Fort Armstrong, earning the honorary title of colonel. After that war, he eventually built his house and operated a booming business. Along with his best friend Antoine LeClaire (below), Davenport founded a number of businesses as well as some towns in the area, including Rock Island, Davenport, and LeClaire. Davenport hosted the first meeting of railroad interests in his home on Rock Island in 1845, beginning the push for the first bridge over the Mississippi. He was murdered in his home on July 4, 1845, just weeks after that meeting.

The first permanent residence on Rock Island, and in the area, was George Davenport's home. Initially a log cabin, Davenport later built a fine house around the old structure. Over time it became a roadhouse, with wings added for a sleeping area and a kitchen. After Davenport's death, the family lived there until after the Civil War.

The Davenport House is seen here around the turn of the 20th century after years of neglect. The Army acquired the home after the Civil War, but it did not use it for long after the core of the arsenal moved to the center of the island. Over the decades, several groups worked to restore the home to its former glory. Today, it is a museum.

This photograph shows the interior of the Davenport house after decades of neglect. Water had penetrated from a neglected roof, and eventually all the plaster collapsed. This room was most likely the living room. Looking beyond the mess, it is evident that this must have been a grand house for the late 1840s on the frontier.

In March 1856, after 11 years of work, the first bridge over the Mississippi opened, using Rock Island as a stepping stone from Illinois to Iowa. The Howe truss bridge was high technology for the day, and the span over the rapids was as long a bridge as was considered feasible in 1856. Overnight, the area became the transportation hub of the United States, combining rail and water routes.

In the early 1860s, an ice floe struck the bridge with such force that the piers moved. The shallow rapids had made it easy to get to bedrock, but, in haste, the designers had not properly sunk the piers into the bedrock. This image shows the damage when the ice pushed piers several feet downriver. Spectators on the shore are seen surveying the damage.

Meanwhile, on the other end of the island, developers in Moline, Illinois, looked to the island as a place to expand. In the back of this 1853 drawing from the Moline bluff, the east end of the island is shown with some development. Moline wanted to expand to take better advantage of the available waterpower.

Plans were developed by David Sears and others to create a subdivision on the island. This map shows an early plan that never came to fruition. The laid-out streets for residential development anticipated sales to residents that never happened, in part because of concerns about ownership of the land. However, the bridge and mill were in place by the mid-1850s.

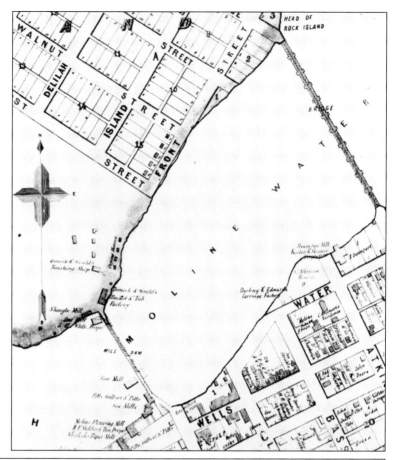

David Sears was the most prolific builder in this early period. He built a dam and a mill, which are seen on the bottom left of the preceding map. His development of waterpower drew other companies to the Moline area, including the John Deere Company. This image shows the mill and dam after the Army bought them.

On the north side of the island, Sears developed another mill and boat landing to include a parallel dam to push more water between Rock Island and the small Benham's Island and bypass the rapids. Sears was paid for his improvements when the Army cleared the island after 1862.

Notice to Trespassers
On the U. S. Reserve on Rock Island.

All persons detected in cutting or destroying Timber on the United States Reserve on Rock Island, will be prosecuted according to the following Act of Congress, passed the 3rd day of March, 1859:

CHAPTER LXXVIII. Be it enacted by the Senate and House of Representatives of the United States, &c. That if any person or persons shall unlawfully cut, aid, or assist, or be employed in unlawfully cutting, or shall wantonly destroy, or procure to be wantonly destroyed, any timber standing, growing, or being upon the lands of the United States, which, in pursuance of any law passed or hereafter to be passed, have been or shall be reserved or purchased by the United States for Military or other purposes; every such person or persons so offending, on conviction thereof, before a Court having competent jurisdiction, shall for every such offence pay a fine not exceeding Five Hundred Dollars, and shall be imprisoned not exceeding Twelve Months.

H. Y. SLAYMAKER, Agent,
July 23, 1860.   **for Qr. M. Dep. U. S. Army.**

As the Army prepared to build facilities on Rock Island, they began to reassert control. The process was not easy and led to extensive litigation. This notice from July 1860 was just part of a campaign to protect government resources on the island and push off squatters. The process was completed after the Civil War.

Two

THE CIVIL WAR ERA

On July 11, 1862, Pres. Abraham Lincoln signed into law a bill creating the Rock Island Arsenal. Despite being created during the war, the first few years of the arsenal were focused not on combat, but instead on construction and housing.

The first commander of the arsenal was Maj. Charles Kingsbury, who had been associated with plans for an arsenal at Rock Island for several years. In May 1863, he was part of a committee dispatched to select the location for the Arsenal buildings on Rock Island. Subsequently, he was appointed commander and charged with building the arsenal. Kingsbury arrived at Rock Island in August 1863 with a plan to construct three buildings intended as a storage and maintenance facility for the Midwest and the frontier. During the course of the next two years, Kingsbury completed the plans and began construction of Storehouse A, which is now called the Clocktower Building. His progress was very slow, with the cornerstone not laid until April 1864. In fact, the building was still not complete when he departed in July 1865.

A variety of problems, including construction stone not being delivered and conflict with the City of Moline, contributed to the delays. However, the larger obstacle was a second military establishment, the Rock Island Prison Barracks. The Prison Barracks was a camp for Confederate prisoners of war. The Prison Barracks had more funding and personnel and tended to divert resources from the arsenal project. Construction began in August 1863, and the first prisoners arrived in December. Eventually, some 12,500 prisoners of war would move through the camp. Just under 2,000 would die, with almost half of that number occurring in the first four months due to extreme cold and smallpox. In addition to the prisoners, the camp saw a large number of Union guards, including the 108th Colored Infantry, a unit of black soldiers deeply hated by the prisoners.

By August 1865, the camp was gone and so was Major Kingsbury. The Clocktower Building remains, but all that is left of the prison camp are the cemetery and photographs.

Maj. Charles P. Kingsbury became the first commander of Rock Island Arsenal in July 1863. A graduate of the United States Military Academy at West Point in 1840, Kingsbury served bravely in the Mexican War and commanded seven other arsenals before taking command at Rock Island. In April 1863, he was the commander of Harpers Ferry Arsenal for just two days. When Virginia militia forces began marching to Harpers Ferry with the aim of capturing some 15,000 rifled muskets, Kingsbury ordered the plant and stocks burned. Some suggest this decision may have saved the Union. Throughout his tenure at Rock Island, Kingsbury agitated to increase the mission to manufacture weapons as a replacement for Harpers Ferry. Apparently, he was eventually seen in Washington as a complainer and was ignored, but when he was replaced in 1865, the first order for the new commander was to build a manufacturing plant. As far as his actual mission, Kingsbury was unable to finish even one building while he was in command at Rock Island Arsenal. (Courtesy of the US Army Sustainment Command History Office.)

The Clocktower Building was the only permanent structure Kingsbury started. A variety of obstacles, including labor and stone shortages, prevented completion during the war. The building was not complete until 1867. At the same time he was overseeing construction, Kingsbury was issuing equipment to the Iowa militia. It appears progress slowed whenever he was not on site.

Unfortunately, there are no surviving construction images of the Clocktower storehouse. Some 400 workers were engaged in construction. The limestone was quarried in LeClaire, Iowa, and delivered by raft and rail. Only the first floor was finished by 1865, when Kingsbury requested reassignment. This image shows the front of the building. The tower side that is most visible is actually the rear.

This 1880s photograph was taken from the guard shack at the main gate to the arsenal. The storehouse was, for an unknown reason, always outside the gates and fences of the main arsenal. It appears that while Kingsbury's successor improved the building, it never played a role in the image of an expanded arsenal after the Civil War.

Perhaps part of the reason for keeping the building outside the gates was because the new 1872 railway bridge had a wagon road and brought many visitors to the island. This image from the 1890s shows tourists on the island. It is probably from after 1896, based on the ladies' apparel.

When Brevet Brig. Gen. Thomas J. Rodman added height to the tower, he also added a clock, purchased from the A.H. Hotchkiss Company. This image shows the main gears. The works sit today in the same place as when they were installed in 1868. The pendulum uses two full stories of the tower. The clock became the time standard for the local area.

Each side of the tower had a clock face. The clockworks precisely drove all four faces. This image shows the drive rod from the central works to one of the faces. The clock also had a chime bell so loud that residents eventually complained, and the Army added mufflers to the striker.

This image is from the 1930s. Looking carefully, the date "1865" is visible over the porte cochere, which was the date Kingsbury expected to finish it. Over time, the Clocktower Building became dilapidated, until the Army Corps of Engineers took it over in the early 1930s. By the time this photograph was taken, the building had been renovated.

This photograph from June 1934 again shows the main entrance to the building. The trees have grown around the structure, making it harder to get a clear view. The building's exterior is essentially unchanged from when it was completed in 1867. Of course, Kingsbury and Rodman never had to plan for car parking around their storehouse.

Kingsbury arrived at Rock Island to find a prisoner-of-war camp being built. It was this camp that competed for labor and other resources. This period bird's-eye view shows not only the camp but also the Clocktower Building and, on the right, the first bridge over the river. The drawing also shows the large complex of buildings for the camp, including prison barracks, guard barracks, administrative buildings, and more.

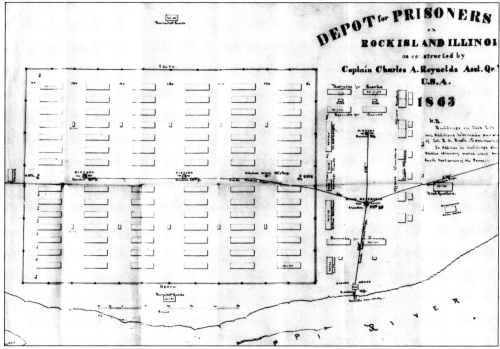

This period drawing shows the main camp layout as constructed by Capt. Charles A. Reynolds. The stockade held 84 prisoner barracks. Outside the stockade, guard barracks were at each corner. On the west side were quarters and administrative areas. Construction started in August 1863, and the first prisoners arrived in December, before the camp was finished. The drawing shows the water system added in 1864.

These images show the west gate. The 12-foot stockade had a walkway several feet down for the guards. Guards are on the walkway, with more Union soldiers on the ground at the guardhouse. The prisoners outside the walls may be new arrivals or a group that has agreed to work outside the stockade for extra pay. Escapes were a constant concern. The image below shows the alarm tower that housed a bell, just outside the gate. In addition to marking routine events during the day, the bell could be rung to call out the guards for escapes or disturbances inside the camp.

This is a street outside the stockade. On the right are quarters for officers. It is unclear if officers' families were able to live in the camp. However, some photographs indicate picket fences and gardens. In the far background is East Davenport, Iowa, to the north across the Mississippi River, where Sioux were held after the 1862 Dakota War in Minnesota.

Other aspects of camp administration included delivery of food and other supplies. The sutler was a civilian contractor paid to provide food but also licensed to sell other goods to the guards and, at times, prisoners. The prisoners were allowed to work for a small wage. This stereographic image shows the sutler's storehouse and other buildings outside the stockade.

In the first three months the camp was open, almost 1,000 prisoners died from smallpox, other infectious disease, and exposure from a brutal winter. In the spring, the Union built a substantial hospital complex. This image shows the last remnants of the camp: a hospital building used as barracks. It was razed in 1909.

Another aspect of the physical complex was administration buildings for the guards. This stereograph shows the headquarters of the 4th Invalid Corps, later called the 4th Veteran Reserve Corps. The Invalid Corps was composed of soldiers who had been wounded and were fit for garrison duty but not combat. These were the first guards at the camp.

Every day, roll was called to ensure prisoners had not escaped or died. This image shows prisoners in front of their barracks during roll call. The guards are also inside the stockade in formation for what was probably a posed photograph. The ditch on the side was either for water circulation or was dug down to bedrock to prevent escape after some enterprising prisoners tunneled out of camp.

Prisoners could be punished for a variety of infractions. Flogging was outlawed, but solitary confinement, thumb screws, and hanging by the thumbs were typical punishments. These prisoners are riding a mule as punishment. The prisoner had to sit on a narrow piece of wood for a prescribed period of time with their feet dangling unsupported. The prisoner in front has his hand on the mule's head.

Several different guard units served at Rock Island, but the unit truly hated by the prisoners was the 108th Colored Infantry, a regiment of former slaves. In a time when the white establishment did not trust blacks in combat, the Army appears to have intentionally assigned blacks as guards in Confederate prison camps to send a message about how norms had changed. This stereograph shows black guards outside the stockade.

Union guards were also subject to discipline. In this image, two black guards are sitting on a mule while another oversees the punishment. In a more positive move, the camp commander, Col. Adolphus Johnson, also built a schoolhouse for the 108th Colored Infantry to teach them reading, writing, and mathematics.

Most punishment described so far was difficult or painful, but there was an ultimate form of discipline for the prisoners. This image shows the "dead line," set four feet inside the stockade wall. Any prisoner crossing the dead line could be shot without warning. While there were incidences of prisoners being shot prior to the arrival of the 108th Colored Infantry, there may have been a short surge after they arrived. It appears the prisoners were so incensed at having black guards that some crossed the dead line to dare the guards to shoot. And shoot they did. In each instance, an investigation was completed that exonerated the guards. Prisoner diaries indicate that the presence of black guards was the single most galling aspect of prison life. In addition to the prisoners, many of the guards died. Some 50 black guards are buried in the Rock Island Federal Cemetery.

At the end of the war, all prisoners had to swear an oath of loyalty to the United States before they could be released. This image shows a group swearing the oath. The last prisoners were released in July 1865. They were transported to the city of Rock Island and were then on their own to get home.

All that remains of the Rock Island Prison Barracks are graves. In addition to the guards in the Federal Cemetery, the Confederate Cemetery holds the remains of 1,961 prisoners. In the late 1880s, a commission was created to ensure the proper accounting of Confederate dead. The commission designed the peaked headstones seen here to make them different from the graves of Federal troops.

Three

THE RODMAN PLAN

In July 1865, Brevet Brig. Gen. Thomas J. Rodman was assigned as the new commander of Rock Island Arsenal. The results of the Civil War had caused a reevaluation of the role of the arsenal. The loss of the manufacturing capacity at Harpers Ferry, and a desire for a manufacturing capacity off the coasts and closer to the frontier led to a revision of the Rock Island Arsenal's role. More than just storage and maintenance, the arsenal was now to be a manufacturing center to support the Army across the nation.

When Rodman arrived, he immediately began to plan the arsenal. He spent a few months evaluating and then developed a plan. Rodman envisioned 10 main shop buildings, backed up with storehouses and offices. But, Rodman did not just plan a plant; he conceived a city with water, bridges, waterpower, barracks, a hospital, homes, and parks. What he designed eventually became reality as the largest American public works project of the 19th century. The federal government spent more money building Rock Island Arsenal than on any other public project.

Rodman began building in 1866. He finished the Clocktower Building and moved on to a water system. At the same time, he began constructing the shops, each covering an acre of land. This required establishing suppliers, hiring labor, and developing local leadership. Fortuitously, Rodman was an anchor of the Ordnance Department and could draw on its resources for talented officers, draftsmen, and supervisors. In 1869, Rodman requested permission to build quarters for the commander, and soon added a housing area.

Unfortunately for the arsenal and the nation, Rodman died in 1871 at the height of his creative and management capacity. His successor, Capt. Daniel Flagler, continued to build Rodman's plan with few major alterations for the next 15 years. The last shop was not completed until 1893, some years after Flagler went on to his next assignment. This chapter shows what Rodman planned and what he, Flagler, and others completed. The story goes forward to the turn of the 20th century, long after Rodman died, but it is still the story of Rodman's plan.

Thomas J. Rodman arrived at Rock Island Arsenal in August 1865. He came from the Boston area, where he had commanded Watertown Arsenal during the Civil War. Rodman was an expert in casting cannons. He had also developed new artillery gunpowder and other technological advancements for the Army. He arrived at the arsenal charged with developing a manufacturing complex, sometimes called a "Grand National Arsenal." This idea had been in play for at least 20 years and was often recommended by the Ordnance and Quartermaster Departments, but, during the Civil War, Congress had become concerned about the vulnerability to foreign attack of the rest of the arsenals on the East Coast. In addition, it was clear that the Army would be active on the frontier after the Civil War. Rodman was charged with creating a plan and then building it. His initial concept was complete by October 1865, and approvals were received early in 1866. By the time he had approvals, Rodman was already at work completing the Clocktower Building. He then rapidly initiated the construction of his master plan.

Rodman moved the arsenal complex to the center of the island in order to take advantage of higher ground and to have enough room for the complex. This move also created some separation and security from the east and west ends of the island, where wagon bridges connected to the Illinois shore. He also moved the railway bridge several hundred yards downriver so the track would run directly past the Clocktower Building. The front gate (above) allowed limited access to those with passes. The cannons were real, but they were more for show than for defense. The photograph below shows the guard on the Moline bridge. This entrance looks much less imposing, but both entrances to the island were protected.

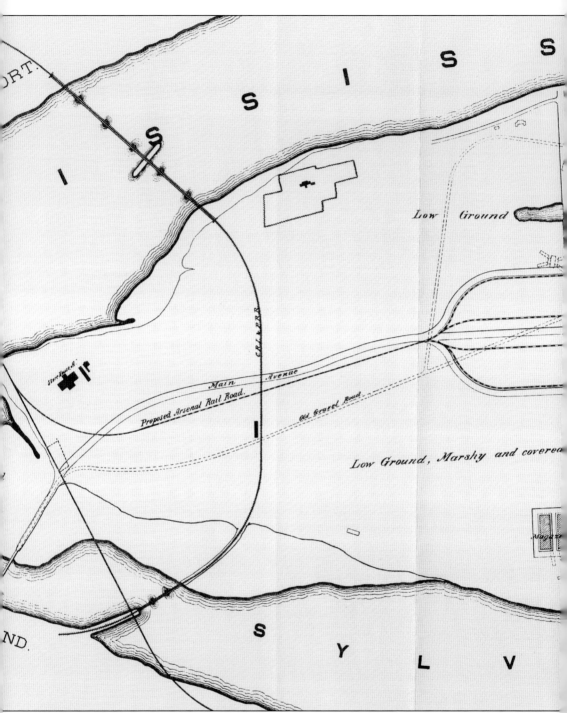

This drawing was included in an 1877 history of the arsenal written by Rodman's successor, Daniel Flagler. While he did not exactly follow Rodman's plan (Rodman himself had changed the waterpower plan and the location of support buildings), Flagler did remain true to the Rodman core during his 15-year command. An interesting aspect of this drawing is that it shows the exact location of the abandoned prisoner-of-war camp, showing that some structures had to be

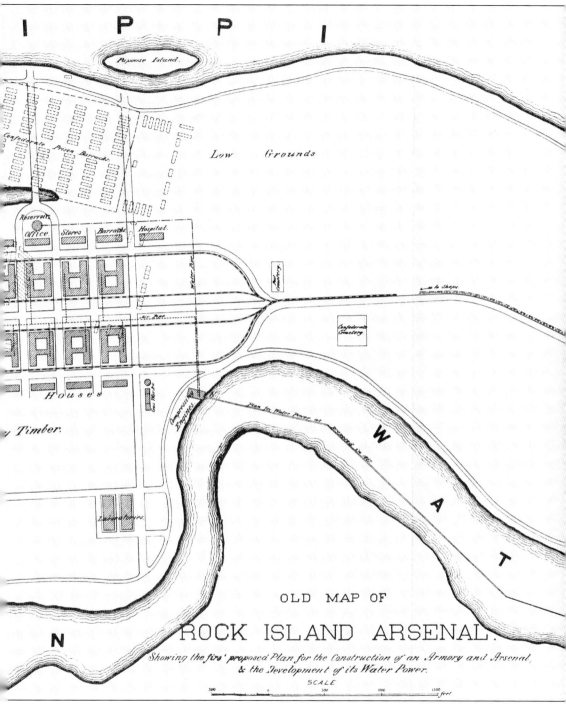

OLD MAP OF

ROCK ISLAND ARSENAL.

Showing the *firs' proposed* Plan for the Construction of an Armory and Arsenal,
& the Development of its Water Power.

SCALE

immediately razed in order to start construction. Some of the old camp buildings were used as temporary housing, storage, and shops. Rodman also added a lake. Not seen on this original plan are the future officers' quarters. The lake was intended as a barrier between residential and industrial parts of the island. (Courtesy of the US Army Sustainment Command History Office.)

Rodman also included a formal post cemetery, added on to the Union Cemetery from the Civil War era. This image shows the gate to the post cemetery. It is uncertain when the gate was built, but, by 1871, Rodman had already begun melting down scrap metal and cannon balls for iron to be used in construction and for fences like the one shown here.

General Rodman died in June 1871, with his building program just begun. Many accounts say that he worked himself to death. About 1,000 people came to his funeral, many of them the countless workers on the project. His obelisk in the post cemetery is flanked by two of the massive Rodman coast defense guns, which he invented.

The first permanent structure of Rodman's own design that was completed was the water reservoir. With water pumped in from the river, the reservoir provided enough constant water under pressure to support construction and early production. The reservoir was designed to hold over one million gallons, but it had to be relined, reducing capacity to 800,000 gallons.

Initially, the reservoir was open. In 1875, a roof was added. Later, a second tower structure was built to provide more pressure. A pump station on the riverbank was built and improved over time. Despite a number of technical difficulties, the reservoir supported the arsenal into the 1970s. It was finally razed in 2010. (Courtesy of the US Army Sustainment Command History Office.)

One of Rodman's first priorities was to move the rail bridge to the west end of the island. Despite having to turn the project over to engineers, his basic plan is seen in the 1872 bridge. This swing-span iron bridge was better placed than the original bridge, with the span on the island side in the natural channel. (Courtesy of the US Army Corps of Engineers Rock Island Library.)

The 1872 bridge was double-decked, with rail on top and a roadbed on the bottom. This view of the upper deck is looking north towards Davenport, Iowa. The huge eagle is missing in other images, and it is not clear whether it was an early or late addition to the structure. The eagle has been lost over time. (Courtesy of the US Army Sustainment Command History Office.)

The road bed on the bottom meant that 1872 was the first time horses, carriages, and wagons did not have to use a ferry to cross the river (the first bridge had a pedestrian walkway). At first, the roadbed was restricted to government use, but in 1873, the Army made the bridge available to all. (Courtesy of the US Army Sustainment Command History Office.)

This image shows the swing span in the open position to allow a steamship through. Smaller craft and log rafts simply went under the spans. The foundation piers were solidly anchored to the riverbed, unlike the 1856 bridge, the piers of which sometimes moved. (Courtesy of the US Army Sustainment Command History Office.)

In addition to the big rail bridge, Rodman also designed a smaller bridge to span the artificial lake he built as a buffer between the residential and industrial areas. The rustic bridge over Crystal Lake provided a roadway to the housing area instead of making people go around. (Courtesy of the US Army Sustainment Command History Office.)

The lake provided a scenic spot for boating and picnics. Unfortunately, it also provided an inviting habitat for mosquitoes. By the mid-1880s the lake was stagnant, and it was drained by 1890. The deteriorating bridge now spans a grassy low spot on the golf course. (Courtesy of the US Army Sustainment Command History Office.)

By the mid-1890s, the iron bridge was obsolete. The single-track 1872 bridge created a bottleneck. A new steel bridge wide enough for two tracks was designed by Ralph Modjeski, one of America's most prolific bridge engineers. The Government Bridge was his first project as chief engineer. The Phoenix Bridge Company executed Modjeski's design. The new bridge opened in 1896.

The new bridge was built around the old bridge so rail traffic could continue to flow. The bridge was actually closed for only a couple of weeks, when the swing span was replaced. This image shows a new span to the right and the old bridge to the left. The rectangular structure is the "Traveler." It moved along the structure, adding the new spans.

Work was delicate and required repeated erection, tear-down, and movement of support structures like the one seen here. The temporary tracks brought a railcar to the side so that iron beams of the old bridge could be removed. The work was also threatened by nature. At least once, parts of the new bridge were rebuilt after ice floes demolished the partially completed span.

This image looks to the west through a new span, with the old 1872 span behind. Partially completed, the track is part of the old span. The double track would be added later. Modjeski's bridge was designed with the most modern safety devices in the structure itself, but the work remained dangerous.

This is the center of the bridge after construction was complete. Both tracks have been laid, and a locomotive is moving across the bridge. In total, the bridge is over 1,600 feet long, with eight spans. The swing span is the longest, at 365 feet. Baltimore trusses make up six of the spans. The other two are Pratt trusses. The swing span weighs over 1,200 tons.

Like the 1872 bridge, the 1896 bridge had a roadway below the rail bed. Supposedly, the road was on the bottom so as to not scare the horses. This is the Davenport entrance. The 1872 bridge had trolley tracks, and the new bridge continued that tradition. Trolleys ran to the arsenal until the 1940s.

This final view of the 1896 bridge and the Clocktower Building was probably taken by Henry Bosse, a Rock Island Corps of Engineers cartographer. Bosse spent time photographing much of the upper Mississippi River. Since he worked at Rock Island, taking this image would have been easy, and the new bridge and old building would have attracted his attention. (Courtesy of the US Army Corps of Engineers Rock Island Library.)

By the time the Government Bridge was completed, the core of the Arsenal was also done. Building the arsenal took much longer than anticipated—some 27 years, from 1866 to 1893. This 1871 photograph is one of the earliest known images of the stone shops and shows Shop B under construction. Shop B was the first building on the north row.

Work proceeded simultaneously on both rows of shops. This 1872 image shows Shop C. In the background, the exhaust chimney is encased in scaffolding. Temporary shops are seen on the left. These shops created materials for construction, including hardware. In essence, the Arsenal started producing immediately in order to build itself.

While this photograph was not taken during the initial construction period, it presents a cross-section of the main shop buildings. Shop H settled, and its east wall cracked. Repairs from 1915 show the outer limestone walls, the vaulted brick fireproof ceilings, and, on the right behind the derrick, the cast-iron stairways made from recycled Civil War cannonballs.

This photograph from around 1875 shows crews of men assembling the truss system for the third floor or attic of the buildings. The main shops had a full basement and three floors, while the foundry and blacksmith shop had only one main level and partial second floors. The iron Fink trusses for the roof eliminated the need for support pillars and created an open bay.

This view of the foundry, also known as Shop E, is probably from the mid-1890s. The foundry and the blacksmith shop looked the same except the blacksmith shop had a smokestack over 100 feet tall. Rodman designed an underground flue system for the forges because he did not want a series of smaller chimneys ruining the roofline. The foundry design must have been near perfect, as the building functioned as a foundry into the 1950s.

Seen here is the blacksmith shop, Shop F, in operation. The dirty, smoky feel of the image probably accurately depicts the air quality in the center of the shops in an age before air filters and scrubbers. Making material for the Army was not a pristine business. Shop F was later converted into a plating shop and held chromium tanks.

This 1878 photograph shows the first couple of races in place as Shop I went up. Note the cranes used to lift the massive limestone blocks into place. Progress slowed in the early 1880s due to budget cuts and problems with late budgets from Congress. Shop I was not completed until 1886, while progress on Shop K lagged another seven years.

This photograph from after 1880 shows a stairwell in Shop H. This design was typical of all the buildings. There were several stairwells in each building, with at least one in each corner of the base and at the end of each leg. The metal was made in the foundry from melted-down excess cannonballs and scrap horseshoes. Brass hardware was made from recycled ammunition components. In addition, support columns were also cast from recycled scrap. In this way, the arsenal has been green since before 1870. The stairwells are still in use today. Unseen in most of these images is that the shops were U-shaped, with a 260-foot base and 300-foot legs. Rodman had discarded the crosspiece seen in the drawing on pages 42–43 in order to create an open courtyard and improve teaming and cooperation among the laborers. Each building sits on about an acre of land.

This Henry Bosse photograph from 1885 or 1886 shows Shop I nearly completed. It also shows something the arsenal was proud of: new trees. Several commanders ensured not only that the island was reforested but also that a wide variety of species were planted. At left is one of the derricks used to lift blocks. (Courtesy of the US Army Corps of Engineers Rock Island Library.)

Pictured in 1911 are the back, or courtyard, sides of the north row of shops. In 1911, these shops would have been phasing down from a decade of making rifles. During World War I, each of the two end shops were connected by walkways so well-built that it is hard to tell they were added up to 45 years after initial construction.

This photograph from 1941 shows one of the storehouses designed to store material and feed it into the shops. Only two were ever built, one of the few instances where Rodman's full plan was not realized. It appears that later commanders realized that the storehouses simply were not needed due to the under-utilization of the entire plant.

This image from before World War I looks east down Main Street (now Rodman Avenue), showing the front facades of the shops. The arsenal used enough stone to erect the massive Joliet limestone shops, but did not pave the streets until much later. The flagpole was moved out of the road during World War I.

This aerial view taken after World War II is a little blurry, but it does show, in one image, the core of Rodman's plan: The U-shaped main shops, the water reservoir, and some housing. It also shows the walkways added during World War I connecting six of the buildings. Behind the shops are a vast array of other buildings added after 1893.

At the same time that he was building the first shops, Rodman also began to harness the power of the Mississippi River to run those shops. This image shows the first dam around 1871. This dam was placed at the narrowest point between the island and the Illinois mainland. The first dams simply created waterpower, turning wheels to mechanically transfer power to the shops.

The system chosen by Rodman to transfer the power was called a Teledyne system. This image shows one of the main towers in 1870. The power wheels in the dam turned wheels with wire cables connecting to the next tower. The cables moved up the slope from the dam towards the shops, then turned down the back of the south row.

This image from the late 1870s shows Shop C in the foreground. The wheel attached to the building transferred the power to a shaft inside the shops. Leather straps then ran the machinery. For another view of the towers and wheels, see page 57. While Rodman intended to power the entire complex, only the south row was ever connected.

By the mid-1890s, the arsenal needed more power. This image from 1889 shows workers excavating and clearing the bed of the slough between Arsenal Island and Sylvan Island in preparation for building a new masonry dam. In the background are the arsenal shops. Temporary coffer dams were erected to drain the water so the bed could be blasted.

This image from 1891 or 1892 shows workers on the river bottom. In this case, the Moline waterfront appears to be in the background. The men are preparing to blast rock. They are using electric drills to bore holes in the rock. Another crew would place explosives in the holes and then wire them to fuzes.

Here is the result of all the work drilling and preparing: a shower of smoke and rock erupts from the blast. After the blast, the crews would return to haul away the debris. This project took from 1889 until 1892 to be completed. Other temporary measures were used to continue powering the shops.

The result of the three-year project was a new masonry waterpower plant with 41 turbine openings. Only eight were ever used. The years after completing the dam were slow years for the arsenal, with work orders dropping significantly. The extra power was simply not needed until the Spanish-American War broke out in 1898.

This 1898 image shows the main shaft inside the dam powerhouse. This shaft drove the Teledyne towers and cables transmitting power from river to shop. Unfortunately, the powerhouse burned in 1899. However, this was the break needed for Congress to authorize a change to hydroelectric power. The new hydroelectric plant, generating 2,500 kilowatts, went online in 1901.

In 1903, the arsenal completed an addition increasing output to 3,150 kilowatts. By World War I, the first hydroelectric plant was considered inefficient. A new addition was abutted to the 1903 dam adding substantially more electric generation after 1919. The arsenal has continued to upgrade the hydroelectric plant over the years. Today, it still produces over 30 percent of the daily power requirement.

Despite the size and scope of the manufacturing shops and waterpower development, Rodman is still best known for the quarters he designed and built beginning in 1869. Quarters No. 1, a National Historic Landmark, was the home for the Arsenal commander. At over 20,000 square feet, it is the largest house in the Army and second only to the White House in the federal inventory.

This 1907 view of Quarters No. 1 is obscured by the trees, but the four-and-a-half-story tower is visible over the third-story roofline. The wraparound porch was perfect for relaxing or entertaining. The house was designed to include family, formal entertaining, and VIP quarters. The third floor, with the small windows, was a hotel for soldiers moving through the area.

The house was designed with central heat, indoor plumbing, hot and cold water, and gas lights. This author believes General Rodman moved into Quarters No. 1 in early 1871 before dying in the house in June of that year. His funeral was the first formal entertaining event. This 1906 view looks at the southwest corner of the house and the large greenhouse, added by 1880.

This 1919 photograph shows the interior of the greenhouse in full bloom. One task disliked by security guards in the winter was having to keep the woodstove in the greenhouse stoked so the commander's plants did not freeze. In addition to the greenhouse, a later commander added a fountain to the south of the house.

In quieter times, the Rock Island Arsenal commander had time to relax. He also entertained on a regular basis with members of the local business community and Army superiors. One can imagine them relaxing in this summer house set on the riverbank. Looking closely reveals the deck that extended over the river flowing 20 feet below.

Rodman also designed smaller quarters, from 6,000 square feet to 7,000 square feet, for his subordinates. Eventually, three were built, and a fourth was added in 1906. All were slightly different. Quarters No. 4 was built in 1872. This image from around 1880 shows a woman and two children, possibly an officer's family, with a carriage and driver. The landscaping is fairly undeveloped.

This early 1900s image shows Quarters No. 2. This set of quarters, constructed in 1872–1873, was about 6,000 square feet. Pictured are two women, a man, and a child on the porch. Unfortunately, their identities are not known. Note the full-length windows that act as doors to the porch. Quarters No. 2, No. 3, and No. 4 are still occupied today.

While not as grandiose as the quarters for officers, the arsenal also had barracks for soldiers. The barracks were constructed in 1873. Designed for 200 soldiers, the barracks included a kitchen, dining areas, and toilets in addition to sleeping bays. The new barracks are seen here in 1873 with young trees. In the front are a soldier and two decorative cannons.

In the 19th century the Army ran on horses, and those workers also needed quarters. The early arsenal had several sets of stables. Seen here in 1898 is a larger set of stables near the barracks. The barn-style building in the back is still used as part of the arsenal's child care services.

One final core building was the combined fire house, police headquarters, and commissary. The building was completed in 1874. This image alone cannot tell the backstory. The stone for this building was quarried near Anamosa, Iowa, by prisoners of the Iowa State Penitentiary. The men lounging in front are probably happy it was not them doing the hard labor. The building is still used for the police and fire departments today.

Four

FIRST CONFLICTS

While the main function of the Rock Island Arsenal in its first 30 years was construction, the installation was also supporting the Army in various ways. At first, the arsenal stored excess equipment and repaired used equipment of all types. In fact, the arsenal operated more as a storage depot than a manufacturing plant. Starting around 1868, almost all equipment for the Army on the frontier was supplied from Rock Island.

In 1875, the arsenal began manufacturing infantry equipment and saddles and other leather products. By 1880, the foundry was making buckles, scabbards, and other metal items. A cloth shop produced haversacks and other canvas goods. In 1882, a tin shop was in full production, making canteens and mess kits. In 1885, the arsenal began metal plating. By 1892, the arsenal was making gun carriages, gun mounts, caissons, ammunition boxes, limbers, and mobile forges.

The Spanish-American War thrust the arsenal into the spotlight in 1898. Telegrams demanded immediate shipment of stored items to the troops gathering for the invasion of Cuba. At the same time, the demand for new items escalated. The workforce grew from less than 700 to almost 3,000 in a matter of months. During the Spanish-American War, the arsenal made a name for itself for quality and speed.

After 1900, the Army realized only about half the shops were in use. Col. Daniel Flagler was now chief of ordnance, and moved to fully engage the plant he spent 16 years building. In 1904, the Army directed that Rock Island manufacture M1903 Springfield rifles. At the same time, Rock Island was recognized as the main production site for the Army's artillery carriages.

When the United States entered World War I in 1917, a new surge of manufacturing orders required increased employment, up to almost 15,000. An ammunition plant was built, along with new artillery production buildings and warehouses. After the armistice in late 1918, excess materials again poured into the arsenal for storage and repair work. This entire period saw a transition from a stable, old-style manufacturing plant to a modern, expandable manufacturing plant able to support the Army in peacetime and at war.

Immediately after the end of the Civil War, the Army flooded Rock Island Arsenal with excess ammunition for storage. This image from before 1870 shows piles of shells and cannonballs in front of some of the temporary shop buildings. It was this type of ammunition that was recycled for brass and iron in support of construction.

In addition to ammunition, artillery pieces were also stored at the arsenal. Eventually, they were organized into gun parks. This image produced in the 1890s shows how the cannon and shot were eventually arranged almost as museum pieces. The careful arrangement probably made it easy to keep track of the inventory. Most of these pieces were never used again and were eventually melted down.

This photograph taken around 1868 is rare because it shows one of the boys hired to work in the ammunition areas. In the middle, a child can be seen sitting on the ammunition. His job was to sprinkle water around the area to keep the powder cool and keep down the dust. Today, it is amazing to think that the youngest employees were used in this most dangerous of jobs. Looking carefully, one can see a variety of ammunition products. The boxes probably contain black gunpowder. The round balls are a variety of sizes. Some are solid, but some have holes drilled in them. These were filled with black gunpowder, making them exploding shot. In the foreground is grapeshot. The case would disintegrate, turning this into a large, shotgun-type blast. At center right is conical shot.

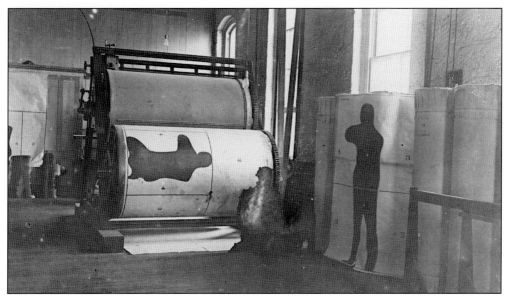

One of the lessons from the Battle of Little Big Horn was that soldiers needed more training in aimed fire. Before 1880, the arsenal was manufacturing targets, and it continues to be the Army's target maker. This is the rotary press, with examples of humans standing and kneeling. They also made targets of horses with riders.

This photograph, while probably taken in 1898, shows some of the early metal manufacturing products. This is a pile of bayonets for the 1873 Springfield rifle. While not yet making rifles, the arsenal made bayonets, scabbards, buckles, slings, and other accessories. These bayonets have been forged and are possibly waiting to be polished.

This picture of employees was taken in 1898 during the Spanish-American War. The men are most likely foremen in a formal posed shot. The man seated second from the right in the first row is David C. Thompson, the first foundry foreman. He began supervising the foundry in 1871 and retired in 1910.

This is one of the milling shops in 1898. These lathes would have been used to turn a variety of metal products. What is remarkable about this image is the complex system of belts and wheels used to turn the lathes. This was before electrification, so all of these lathes ran off of waterpower through the Teledyne system.

These men are skilled craftsmen working on stocks for carbines for the 1873 Springfield rifles in one of the woodshops. While the Army had the Krag rifle by 1898, it did not have enough for the reserve forces and had to issue obsolete 1873s. The older man at right appears to be moving a wheelbarrow full of scrap stocks.

This is part of a series of photographs taken during the Spanish-American War. The gun carriages were a major function of the arsenal after 1890. The arsenal manufactured a wide variety of sizes. These are likely for the 3.2-inch field gun, model 1895 or 1898. The arsenal wheelwrights made the sturdy wheels needed to take the pounding of field use.

This 1898 image shows the construction of boxes for artillery caissons. The caissons were pulled behind the artillery piece and carried ammunition, fuzes, and other supplies. In all, an artillery set consisted of the gun, the caisson, ammunition boxes, and limbers harnessed to the horses. Everything except the actual cannon tube was made at the arsenal.

This is a model 1898 seven-inch siege gun, pictured in 1898. This must have been one of the first produced by the arsenal and then rushed off to the front. The carriage and trails—the pieces holding the tube—are all metal. This was a major shift forward from mainly wooden carriages. The worker leaning on the heavy-duty wheel gives some scale.

In 1898, a gun tube has just been mounted onto its carriage. The winch was needed to lift the heavy tube. This is another example of the iron carriages manufactured by the arsenal, primarily using rivets, not welding. The wheels in the back were taken off when the gun was prepared to fire.

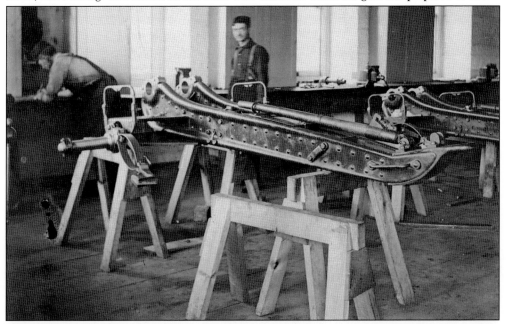

This 1898 photograph shows a gun carriage being manufactured in the assembly shops. The riveted assembly of the carriage is clearly visible, as are the axles and a very rudimentary spring system. None of the guns used in the Spanish-American War had recoil systems, so the carriage and wheels had to absorb all the shock of firing.

Arsenal craftsmen did not just make heavy carriages from metal. They also worked extensively in tin to make all of the products shown in this 1898 image. Knives, forks, spoons, mess kits, and cups were all made in the tin shop. Many of the items were made by stamping out tin sheets.

This is the final stage of manufacturing canteens, pictured in 1898. The workers are adding a stopper, cloth cover, and straps. This must have been tiring, repetitive work. This employee looks exhausted. The arsenal commander was authorized to add shifts and overtime work during the war.

Not only did the arsenal make the mess kit a soldier used to eat meals, they also made the tin cans used to pack the food. Seen here in 1898 is another part of the tin shop where the workers seem to be only making tin cans of various sizes. These would be shipped to a canning factory to add the food.

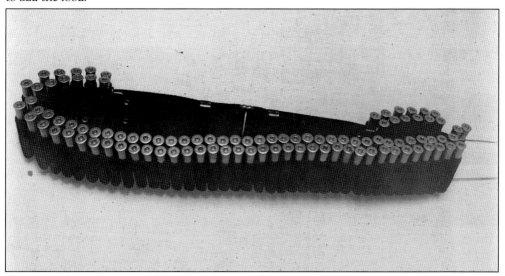

Working with a softer material, the cloth shops made a wide variety of products, including canteen cases, straps, and haversacks. This is a Rock Island belt with the bullets added, pictured in 1898. These are .45-caliber bullets used in the obsolete 1873 Springfield rifles issued to the reserves. The arsenal also made .30-caliber cartridge belts for the regulation Krag rifles.

Transportation was key to the arsenal, as products had to be shipped. This image shows a mix of local and national transportation. The boxes contain .45-caliber pistol ammunition. The arsenal did not make ammunition at that time, but probably stored rounds and shipped them as part of the depot operation. The bicycles represent the modern form of worker transport in 1898.

This 1898 photograph shows the final step in the process: shipping items to the front. These men are mounting gun carriages onto flatbed railcars of the Chicago–Rock Island line. This image reinforces the importance of the rail bridges over the Mississippi in selecting Rock Island as the location for a major arsenal. No gun tubes are present, so these may be replacements.

When the Spanish-American War ended, production slowed, but repair and refurbishment work continued at a steady pace. This photograph from around 1900 shows a rail load of cannons and caissons returning to Rock Island from Cuba. This is just a small portion of the many items sent back to the arsenal for repair and long-term storage.

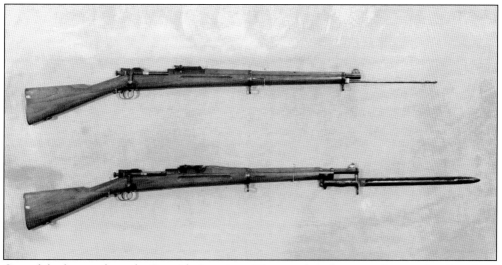

One of the lessons from the Spanish-American War was that the arsenal was only using about half its capacity. The War Department decided to direct production of the Model 1903 Springfield rifle to Rock Island. In 1904, production began. This 1905 image shows two variants made at the arsenal. Arsenal metallurgists developed superior alloys over the original design.

Congress had allocated funding for a small arms plant at Rock Island Arsenal in 1899. Modern machinery was purchased in 1900 or 1901 and installed by 1903. This undated photograph shows the Pratt-Whitney lathes installed in Shop B, today's Building 60. These were used on the tedious process of rifling the barrels. In 1904, Rodman's plan for an armory was finally realized.

The rifle-manufacturing process made every part of the M1903, from the barrel to the wood stock. Pictured here in 1904 is the shop that made the rifle stocks. This operation was in Shop D, today's Building 62. The M1903 Springfield was produced until 1912, and then again during World War I.

The new rifle production required new officers to manage the plant. Quarters No. 6 was built in 1905 for the new plant manager. This 8,000-square-foot house has rich wood and Palladian windows. Completed in 1906, Quarters No. 6 was the first home on the island designed to operate with electricity. This reflects the conversion of the dam to hydroelectric operations in 1901.

The arsenal managed to upgrade other areas in the early 1900s. This 1905 image from an *American Machinist* magazine article on the arsenal shows the new equipment in the harness shop. Rows of cutters, stampers, and sewing machines fill the shop. At top left, the electrical wires added after 1901 are visible.

Cannon work continued in the early 1900s, as seen here in 1908. Men are mounting cannons to carriages in the basement of Shop I, today's Building 110. While there had not been any further development of the cannon, there was now electric light. The water pipes hanging from the ceiling may be an early fire suppression system.

Fire was always a concern, especially after introducing electricity to the shops. A 1904 fire severely damaged one wing of Shop I. This photograph of the 1904 fire shows workers evacuated from the building. An arsenal fire wagon can be seen in the courtyard. A formal fire department was not formed until World War I.

In the early 1900s, the arsenal also adapted to the internal combustion engine for shops and transportation. While horse power continued to be the main transport method prior to World War I, the arsenal did purchase some automobiles. This undated photograph, probably from around 1910, shows an official arsenal car with a winter cover.

In the pre–World War I period, photographers started taking posed pictures of groups of arsenal employees. The photographic record up until then tended to be of the buildings or small groups of employees at work. This image from around 1909, however, shows a group posing in front of the water reservoir. Due to its proximity, the men are probably from one of the rifle shops.

The workers in the previous photograph probably could not afford to be a member of the Rock Island Arsenal Golf Club. Founded in 1894, the club was soon a place for the prominent businessmen. While the arsenal commander, beginning with Colonel Blunt, was always the president, the golf course was a private club leasing public land until 2010. The new clubhouse is seen here in 1906.

In the early 1900s, the arsenal was also a place for local citizens to walk, picnic, and enjoy the scenery, just as the Native Americans had before the Americans arrived. This undated image, probably from the Western View Company, shows three women posing at one of the gun storage parks. Some captured Spanish cannons arrived after 1900, and the storage facilities were improved.

In 1917, the United States joined World War I. Rapidly, the labor pool grew from around 2,000 to almost 15,000. Women who may have only come to Rock Island Arsenal to pose on cannons, or perhaps to work as a secretary, were suddenly called to patriotic work. Not only did the workforce have to expand, but men who might have held those jobs were drafted into the Army. For the first time, women worked as skilled laborers in traditionally male jobs. By 1918, they made up 10 percent of the workforce. For the first time, African Americans were also hired in other than construction and janitorial work, though they still tended to be employed as unskilled manual labor. Women's dress was a particular concern to the arsenal commander, who was afraid that the sight of the female form would distract male workers. In response, he designed a fairly shapeless sateen uniform. Women who worked with machinery were given a little leeway to wear less baggy uniforms.

In 1918, three women wearing the regulation uniform are star gauging a barrel. Star gauging is an inspection to determine if a barrel is the right length and the correct diameter the entire length of the barrel. If there were variations, often caused by improper rifling, they could reject the barrel. This is probably in the rifle manufacture shops.

185-31692 12-30-18
View of Girls at R. I. A.
Star Gauging.

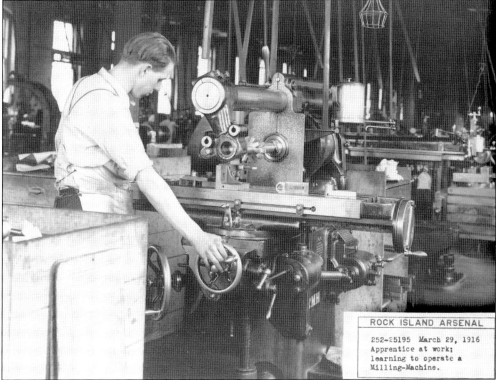

ROCK ISLAND ARSENAL

252-25195 March 29, 1916
Apprentice at work;
learning to operate a
Milling-Machine.

A large number of new male employees were also hired to meet demand. The arsenal had to create a compressed apprenticeship program to develop enough machinists and skilled labor. Most of the highly skilled jobs were still held by men. In 1916, this apprentice is learning how to mill metal shapes.

For the most part, the new war saw the same kinds of items being made as during the last war, with the exception of the M1903 rifles. Artillery continued to be the main production item for the arsenal. However, with demand skyrocketing, shops began to get cramped. Pictured here in 1918, trails are being assembled for 75-millimeter guns.

In this 1918 photograph, carriages for 75-millimeter guns are being assembled. Again, the conditions are much more cramped than they had been in 1898, with more workers producing more carriages. Essentially, the arsenal had run out of flexibility. It is interesting to see the number of US flags hung throughout the shops. The meaning of the stripes on the columns has been lost.

In 1917 and 1918, the arsenal was at full capacity for the first time, with every stone shop fully engaged. The arsenal began a vast program of new construction. One of the first new buildings was the Field and Siege Shop, shown here in early 1918. The style of architecture was vastly different than the Rodman Plan, with a more spacious and well-lit work area to accommodate larger equipment.

This 1918 photograph shows the interior of the main craneway in the new Field and Siege Shop filled with a variety of items produced and repaired by the arsenal in World War I. Compare this image to the earlier photographs of artillery work in the old stone shops. This huge and airy space was big enough for the larger guns being developed.

The arsenal worked on a variety of guns during World War I. Some of the American-developed guns were obsolete by the time the United States entered the war. The carriage on this three-inch gun mounted an oil-and-spring-based recoil system. When fired, the gun jumped and had to be re-aimed, especially if the recoil was oblique to the trails.

Pictured in 1912, this is a Rock Island–developed 4.7-inch gun carriage, recoil, and trails. This was also a spring-and-oil-based recoil. The French 75-millimeter used a hydro-pneumatic recoil. The oil and air system created a much softer recoil, leaving the gun on target no matter what angle it was fired from. Rock Island eventually was licensed to build the recoil, but it could not get any made before the war ended.

With so much artillery being produced and issued to the Army in training (very little American artillery actually made it to France), the arsenal needed a new building to store carriages and parts. This resulted in the construction of Storehouse W1 in 1918 and 1919 by Walsh Construction Company. This is the completed six-story building in 1921.

The only really new product produced in World War I was 155-millimeter artillery ammunition, which required an entirely new building and storage areas for explosives. Shop L, now Building 250, was constructed in 1918 and immediately put into use. The arsenal filled shells made elsewhere, and also made fuzes. After the war, this building was immediately converted to machine shops and never used for ammunition again.

In July 1918, workers are filling shells with explosives. This is a low-tech operation. The TNT was melted in kettles, transferred to buckets, and then poured into the shell. The handwritten notes explain that the rooms behind are "bomb proof," where someone had to clean the hardened TNT out of the shell threads so a cap could be screwed in place.

This interesting July 1918 image shows a different part of the pour room. The melting kettles are to the left. Note the African American workers. These workers were never included in any of the official published photographs of the operation and were edited out in the 1920s to show an all-white crew. There were also black women working in the ammunition plant.

This December 1918 photograph shows white female employees at the ammunition plant. The women were employed in the fuze room, where they worked with mercury fulminate, an unstable explosive mixture sensitive to shock and heat. It was thought that the women who did needlepoint had enough dexterity to work with the sensitive explosive mixture.

Unfortunately, mercury fulminate is unstable. Seen here in December 1918 are the results of an accidental explosion. The windows blew out, the ceiling came down, and a hole was blown through the concrete floor. The plant was made with much glass so that in an explosion, the windows would blow out instead of the walls. No serious structural damage was done, and there is no report of any women being killed.

Not all was hard work and danger at the arsenal during World War I. This 1918 photograph shows the championship baseball team. The team name, Armory, suggests that these players worked in the rifle production shops. Arsenal teams competed on the island and also in various city leagues in Rock Island, Moline, and Davenport.

This final image of the 1865–1918 period shows workers on their way home on a dreary, wet afternoon. While walkers and bicyclists are dominant, now there are also automobiles and a trolley system, which was allowed on the arsenal to reduce traffic. By 1918, the arsenal had proven itself. What was unknown was the aftermath of the "war to end all wars."

Five

THE INTERWAR PERIOD AND WORLD WAR II

World War I ended in November 1918, with Rock Island Arsenal in full swing. While employment levels dropped almost immediately, and most of the women workers were let go, the residual effects of the war continued for several years. Massive amounts of excess material arrived, and buildings were erected to house it all. The arsenal shifted from production back to repair and refurbishment.

While some might consider the excess equipment and associated construction projects a continuation of World War I, this author tends to think of it as the start of the interwar period and the transition to World War II. Work on the excess, learning to make the French recoil system, and developing modern equipment with modern tools and modern buildings are a leap to the future, not a look back to World War I.

At the same time, Rock Island Arsenal began to develop new items for the Army. Much work was done on machine guns, automotive engines, armored cars, and tanks. Rock Island Arsenal made the first American tanks in 1919–1920 and was the tank development center for the Army until 1939. The arsenal also developed tractors and self-propelled artillery, all meant to create a modern Army.

The arsenal rebounded from the postwar cuts and the Great Depression by the early 1930s. By 1937, the arsenal was engaged in new production, and began producing for our soon-to-be allies after September 1939. By the time the United States entered World War II in December 1941, the arsenal thought it was in full swing. It was not even close. By 1943, almost 19,000 employees were engaged and the arsenal hummed 24 hours a day. Over 30 percent of the workforce was women, working in every shop on the island.

In late 1945, the arsenal was reducing staff and output, but leadership felt that they had again proven their worth. They had; however, 1945 was a heyday the Rock Island Arsenal would never again see.

As soon as World War I was over, Rock Island Arsenal was flooded with excess equipment, parts, and material. Over 3,000 railcar loads arrived in 1921. The wave of equipment rapidly overwhelmed the available storage space. This photograph from 1919 shows dozens of French 75-millimeter guns stored outside because covered storage was unavailable.

Pictured here in 1924 is the XYZ area that was built south of Shops G and I during the war. These were initially intended as storage areas for nitrates and ammunition. However, at the end of the war, the ammunition plant was immediately converted to machine shops. The XYZ buildings were converted from ammunition supply storage to storage for excess material.

On the island's west end, more storage areas were added. Seen here, probably during World War II, is the West Storage Area, constructed in the early 1920s to store artillery components. In addition to this construction, Rock Island stored large amounts of material at Savanna Proving Grounds, some 60 road miles north along the Mississippi River. Most of the equipment was obsolete before it was ever needed again.

While most of the old equipment became obsolete, the arsenal was a hotbed of technological innovation from 1920 until World War II. Modern weapons and methods were developed. This is perhaps symbolized by the visit of Charles Lindbergh in August 1927. Lindbergh stayed at Quarters No. 1 and was feted at a formal dinner on the island. He is pictured here at left with Col. David King.

One technological innovation was the opening of a lock and dam at Rock Island in March 1932. The lock and dam raised the river up to 20 feet around the island, obscuring the famous rapids. This was the first lock and dam of the 1930s project to be completed. This photograph from 1934 shows the lock and dam from the top of the Clocktower Building. (Courtesy of the US Army Corps of Engineers Rock Island Library.)

An older throwback showed up soon after. The Trinity River admiral, B.M. Hatfield (left), made an appearance in June 1934 to receive a sample of water from the Mississippi. In 1933 and 1934, Hatfield and his ship, the *Texas Steer*, collected water from 24 different streams between Grand Prairie, Texas, and Chicago. (Courtesy of the US Army Corps of Engineers Rock Island Library.)

Closer to its past strength, the arsenal spent the interwar period modernizing artillery. The arsenal moved carriage design forward from what was seen in World War I to the modern artillery that saw heavy use in World War II. Most of the work was complete a year before the Unites States joined the war. Pictured here in September 1941 is the towed M1 4.5-inch gun.

This image shows the similarity in design of the differently sized artillery pieces. This is an M1 155-millimeter towed howitzer configured for travel, pictured in September 1941. All of the pieces developed in the interwar period had modern, hydro-pneumatic recoils. While the arsenal did work in self-propelled artillery, that work culminated late in the war.

This is the even larger M1 eight-inch howitzer. Development began in 1940, and the gun was in limited production in early 1942. It could throw a shell over 18 miles. The 155-millimeter howitzer had a range of over 9 miles, while the 4.5-inch gun had a range of about 12 miles.

This final image of artillery development shows the famous M2 105-millimeter howitzer. This gun was a mainstay weapon of the war. With a range of just under seven miles and a weight of only 5,000 pounds, this gun went anywhere the Army did. Over 8,500 were produced by the arsenal. These M2s are pictured ready to ship to Great Britain in April 1941.

Another important line of research and development for the arsenal came in a new field. In 1919, the arsenal assembled the first American tank, the Mark VIII. While the arsenal was intended to be a place to assemble parts made elsewhere, the arsenal had to modify many of the parts and make others new. This is a side view of a completed tank in 1919.

Despite these kinds of challenges, the arsenal produced 100 tanks in just 286 days. Seen here in December 1919, one of the tanks is being assembled in Shop M. Based on the success of completing the order on time and the demonstrated ability to make parts in the shops, Rock Island Arsenal became the Army's tank development center.

Over the next 20 years, the arsenal pushed American tank development from the American-British joint venture Mark VIII to the all-American tanks that started World War II. The progress was dramatic from the Mark VIII forward. This photograph from the early 1930s shows a series of M1 combat cars on parade with the Clocktower Building in the background.

The Army soon realized that only having mounted machine guns was a disadvantage. Soon, Rock Island developed the M2 Light Tank, and the name "combat car" was abandoned. This 1937 image shows a M2A2 Light Tank on a test track. Look at the difference from the Mark VIII. The M2A4 Light Tank saw action with the Marines in the Pacific.

Rock Island soon developed a heavier tank based on the light tanks. This resulted, in 1939, in the M2 Medium Tank. However, just as the new tank entered production, events in Europe demonstrated that its light armament and thin armor would not allow it to compete with European tanks. The M2 Medium Tank saw extensive service as a trainer.

Design for the M3 Medium Tank began in early 1940, and production began by the end of the year. This tank mounted a 75-millimeter gun in a sponson. The first made were immediately shipped to the British and saw service in North Africa before the United States joined the war. This was the last tank developed by Rock Island. The next were designed in Detroit.

By late 1939, orders flowed into the arsenal to be sent to our future allies. The Army also got ready to enter the war, and production and manpower began to ramp up. This 1938 photograph shows the craneway of Building 220 full of activity. In two years, it would be full of M2 and M3 tanks. The arsenal was ready for World War II.

As production heated up, space became tight. Everything on the arsenal grew in a matter of weeks after December 7, 1941, and shops became crowded. This is the forge shop in 1942. It is a wonderful snapshot of the activity, with many machines and people crammed into a small workspace.

Other areas also became overfilled with people and machines. This 1941 view of the blacksmith shop again reflects the growth in the first months of the war. Employment eventually reached almost 20,000. As new employees came on, the shops went to three shifts to allow enough space and meet demand.

As funds began to flow, the arsenal was able to upgrade to modern, higher-capacity equipment. While there were more new machines, they were often also larger, to create bigger and bigger parts and assemblies for modern weapons. In this June 1942, Col. C.A. Waldman makes the first piece on a new forge hammer.

Even the old spaces were made new. Shop L, the ammunition plant in the last war, was closed by 1925, but it reopened in 1938 as orders ramped up. Now it was also filled with new machines, even though the space had not been designed for this kind of work. This December 1940 photograph shows some of the new lathes.

All of those employees had to eat. However, there was no space for a cafeteria in the shops, and foremen did not want the workers to have to walk to the central cafeteria. This image from 1943 shows the World War II equivalent of the modern "roach coach." The food came to the workers.

The arsenal also created training schools for soldiers and civilian technicians. The civilian technicians would be sent to units in training or in the field to teach about new equipment and troubleshoot problems. Space was so tight that training on light weapons took place in attics, as seen here in 1943.

Even the parking and traffic were worse. Gone were the horses and bicycles. Now, most workers had a car that they wanted to drive to work and park. Buses and trolleys still serviced the island, but the huge growth in employees caused traffic jams at shift changes, as seen in this undated photograph.

Fortunately, leadership had realized early the new requirements and made plans for new construction. On June 1, 1942, construction began on a new massive shop, Building 208. Before January 1943, the building was occupied and in use. To get a feel for the size, the cars coming from the right in the previous image are in the gap between the two farthest buildings in this image.

This is one of the main production bays in Building 208 in July 1943. Employees are working on 4.5-inch and 155-millimeter howitzers. The equipment and workers are dwarfed by the size of the bay. Production-line operations could be established in the new building.

Artillery work continued on an expanded scale in the new shop. In July 1943, the production staff is testing interchangeable parts on the improved M1 155-millimeter Long Tom artillery piece in a different part of Building 208. Obviously, as the shops grew, the equipment grew larger as well.

Machine shops were established in other parts of the new building, allowing a thinning out of some of the older, more cramped spaces. In this 1943 photograph, a massive new seven-inch boring mill is being installed in Shop M, in space freed up by moving operations to Building 208. This machine could mill steel castings weighing up to 22 tons.

This final view of large manufacturing was captured in late 1945. It shows production line refurbishment of M4 Medium Tanks as the war effort drew to a close. In total, approximately 7,000 gun carriages were made and assembled, over 20,000 recoil mechanisms were made, and over 10,000 heavy weapons were refurbished in the course of the war.

Not all was hard work. Management understood that it had an interest in helping employees relax and maintain their morale. Despite the cramped conditions, the arsenal leadership managed to find space in the basement of Shop B to construct a six-lane bowling alley. Parts of three lanes are seen here during the war years.

Luckily, there was always time and space for athletes on a ball diamond. This September 1943 photograph shows the Rock Island Arsenal Soft Ball Club. A notation on the back says that the team was the Davenport Diamond Ball League and city champions. Maj. Frank W. Smith, in uniform at center, was the military sponsor.

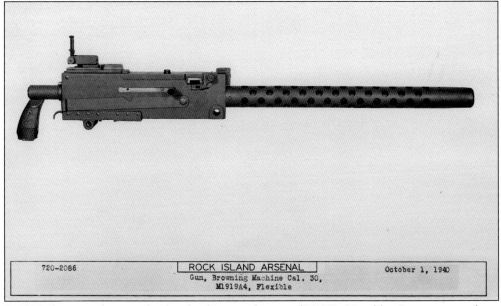

720-2086   ROCK ISLAND ARSENAL   October 1, 1940
Gun, Browning Machine Cal. 30,
M1919A4, Flexible

In 1938, the arsenal received orders for the manufacture of M1919 .30-caliber Browning machine guns. These guns were made in a variety of configurations. This production image from 1940 shows the M1919A4 configuration. This mass production of machine guns was another new mission for the arsenal and was important for many reasons.

William Baumbeck is pictured at his desk in 1942 or 1943. Baumbeck became the arsenal's top civilian employee in 1926 and remained as the senior supervisor until he retired in 1946. In 1936, he invented the broaching method of rifling barrels. This invention made possible the mass production of rifle and machine gun barrels.

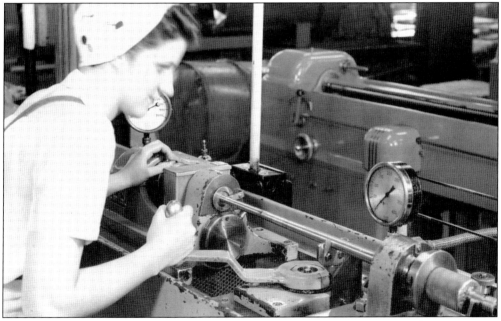

The new broaching method increased production of rifle barrels from three per hour to over 30 per hour. The first machine gun barrel was broach rifled in 1940. This female employee is working at a broaching machine in April 1943. During the war, rifling was done completely by women. The picture is obviously posed, as there is no pressure on the gauges.

Women were first hired to production jobs in June 1942. They rapidly displaced most of the men in the machine gun manufacture shops. These women are manufacturing various parts for the Browning .30-caliber machine guns in Shop K in January 1943. Note that there are no special uniforms like there had been in the previous war.

This photograph from April 1943 shows that not only were black women hired, but, during this war, they were also not kept in unskilled jobs or in the shadows. The war was a great opportunity for women and people of color in federal employment. These ladies, Wanda Nelson and Gertrude Akins, are making covers for the machine guns.

Pictured here in January 1943 is the final inspection line. Women's equality only went so far—the inspectors were all men. True equality would not come until the 1980s and 1990s. During the war, Rock Island Arsenal manufactured 84,587 .30-caliber machine guns. In addition, they made another 700,000 machine gun barrels.

As noted before, arsenal management looked for ways to entertain the workforce and keep up their morale. This is the Rock Island Arsenal girls' chorus, under the direction of Margaret Hall. These ladies, many of them probably from the machine gun shop and the supply depot, performed on Arsenal Island and in the local communities.

Speaking of arsenal leadership, they were also squeezed by the growth and the tight conditions. The commander's office had been in one of the shops in the late 1920s, but was occupying valuable space by the late 1930s. This photograph taken after the war shows the new headquarters building built in 1942 to house the commander and the army of administrators needed to run the arsenal.

The Rock Island Ordnance Depot, the supply operation of the arsenal, was also squeezed in 1940. Like the production shops, inventory and requests started to grow after 1936 and became a tidal wave by 1939. This photograph from around 1942 shows the cramped quarters and dark conditions inside Warehouse 1, the huge warehouse built during the last war.

In response, in April 1941, seven months before the United States entered the war, the arsenal began erecting a new supply warehouse that was, when complete in April 1942, the largest ordnance storehouse in the world. The massive building, large enough to house 17 football fields, is pictured here after the war.

Pictured in August 1942 is the interior of the center bay that ran the length of the warehouse. Two rail spurs entered the building for easy and secret unloading. A total of 18 storage wings ran out perpendicular to each side of the center bay. Here, a light tank and mule tractors can be seen on the platform.

The warehouses were busy 24 hours a day storing, pulling, and shipping repair parts and supplies to units in the United States, Europe, and the Pacific. Gaining a job as a forklift operator or mule driver was a great plum, because you did not have to walk in the warehouses. This photograph from 1944 shows a black female driver picking up a load.

Besides making artillery, tanks, and machine guns, the arsenal also developed some less-recognized projects. World War II saw the first significant use of paratroopers. The Army soon learned that paratroopers often had to be resupplied by parachute. In just a few months, in 1942, the arsenal developed the paracrate. These were sturdy, air-droppable cases filled with supplies. The developers of the paracrates are seen here in February 1945 with samples.

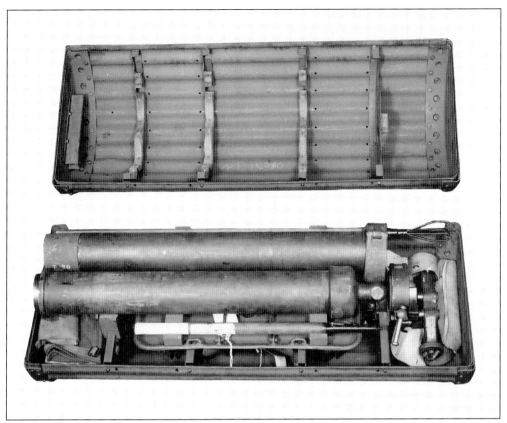

Paracrates were made to airdrop ammunition, general supplies, small arms, and a variety of larger weapons. This August 1944 sample picture shows a paracrate designed to hold parts of a 105-millimeter mortar. Other crates would have delivered the rest of the weapon and the ammunition. Over 6,000 paracrates were made and delivered to the troops.

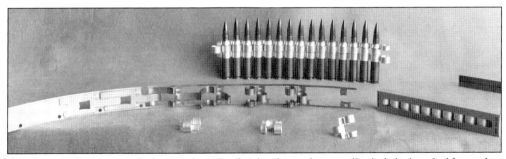

Another small but critical item made at Rock Island was the metallic belt link to hold together belts of machine gun ammunition. The links were developed to replace cloth belt systems used in World War I. Shown here is the process from sheet metal to completed links. The arsenal made over 190 million links.

For all of its efforts, Rock Island Arsenal was awarded the coveted Army-Navy "E" pennant less than a year into the war. Seen here in September 1942, the man on the far right is Brig. Gen. Norman F. Ramsey, commander of the arsenal for most of the war. Rock Island Arsenal—its buildings, machines, and people—did its part to win the war of materiel.

This final image from the World War II period shows employees gathered in the craneway of Shop M, Building 220, to hear the news of Germany's surrender on May 8, 1945, and observe a moment of silence. After over eight years of increased and sustained production, the job was almost done. On August 14, the Japanese would also surrender, but by then, the arsenal was already well along to returning to peacetime operations. Reduction of employees had started in late 1944. Many product lines were suspended in early 1945. Just five days after Japan surrendered, the arsenal returned to a 40-hour workweek. By early 1946, employment was down to under 1,500. Perhaps they did not realize it then, as they only hoped for an end to war, but Rock Island Arsenal had seen its heyday. While remaining critical to the defense of the United States, the arsenal would never again be as big or as busy as it was in late 1944.

Six

INTO THE ATOMIC AGE

When World War II was over, the Rock Island Arsenal quickly reverted to peacetime operations. As employees were let go, production orders were finished or cancelled. Excess machinery and material from civilian producers arrived and was stored. Lingering construction projects were completed. It was good that so much construction had occurred during the war, because it was the last major construction until the 1980s. In 30 years, what had been modern was obsolete.

Despite the lack of modernization of the plant, the arsenal continued to develop new projects that supported the Army during the Cold War. The arsenal helped develop recoilless rifles, improved bazookas, and modern towed and self-propelled artillery. In addition to artillery and machine guns, the engineers and shops developed new items that supported atomic weaponry. While the arsenal had, in a very secret project, developed the metal bomb bodies and some electronics for the atomic bombs used to end World War II, in the postwar period, it worked on artillery and missile systems that could deliver atomic devices for the Army. Some of those projects look less rewarding now than they must have in the late 1950s.

The arsenal also continued to improve its test and engineering processes and facilities. Beginning with new test labs started during World War II, the later-named Rodman Labs continued to expand as the arsenal needed modern research and development facilities. This work resulted in the Ware Simulation Center on the east end of the island. That test center continues to provide support today.

Finally, toward the end of the Cold War, the Army invested several hundred million dollars in modernizing the plant. Construction started in 1982 and was complete in 1988. This project, called Renovation of Armament Manufacturing, or REARM, made the arsenal the most modern manufacturing complex in the US military and resulted in the last production moving out of the old stone shops.

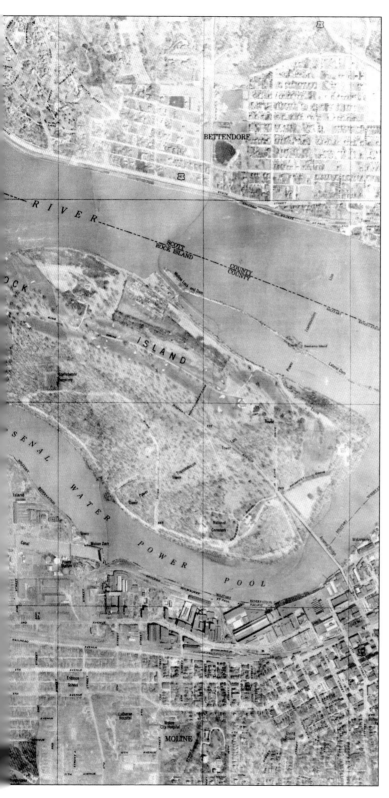

This aerial view from 1954 shows the entire island and gives a snapshot of all the construction and change since 1862. Looking closely, all of the buildings and the main roads are labeled. Unfortunately for modernization, this is how the island continued to look until the mid-1980s. Despite larger weapons and the shift to rocketry, work was done in the same buildings, including the stone shops. Actual square footage was never an issue, as employment levels only hit about 7,000 during the Korean War and about the same during Vietnam—nowhere close to World War II's 19,000. Over time, more white-collar work developed, and many shops and warehouses were converted to office space.

Rock Island had already begun work on lightweight rocket systems in World War II, including manufacturing the bazooka. These engineers are working on a modern variation of soldier-fired antitank weapons in 1955. This appears to be an upgrade of the Korean War bazooka. Note the cast columns in the background, showing that this was in one of the old stone shops.

The arsenal also developed larger, recoilless rifles. This image from the early 1950s shows a Battalion Anti-Tank Gun (BAT) on an M38 Jeep. This weapon and many variations of it were used by the US army, and many allies, well into the 1970s. In addition to adding this gun onto Jeeps, the arsenal also converted Jeeps to ambulances in the same time period.

The arsenal's engineering staff slowly developed more modern test centers. This undated photograph shows the Ware Simulation Center, probably in the mid-1960s. The buildings in the foreground were constructed during World War II, and those in the background were added later. Eventually, the center could mount and test artillery and helicopter-mounted weapons without having to actually fire a shot.

From small to large, the arsenal also worked on new heavy artillery. Pictured here in 1953 is the M65 Atomic Cannon. This 280-millimeter artillery piece could throw a conventional or nuclear shell about 20 miles. Two trucks picked up, moved, and emplaced the massive gun system. Rock Island developed the gun mounts and carriage. The gun was deployed in 1953 and remained in service until 1963. Only 20 were manufactured.

One of the most interesting items ever worked on at the arsenal was the Davy Crocket. This was a nuclear-tipped infantry weapon. The gun came mounted on a tripod or on a Jeep. In this 1961 photograph, the M29 has the spotting rifle attached. Rock Island designed the mount and spotting rifle. The Davy Crocket was fielded in 1961 and stayed in service in Europe and South Korea until 1971.

11-070-1141-62536	ROCK ISLAND ARSENAL ORDNANCE CORPS	April 28, 1959
	Davy Crockett Type B Weapons System. Weapon on carrier in traveling position, side.	

This 1959 image shows a scale model of a mounting concept with a stick figure for scale. It is hard to imagine a nuclear weapon on what looks like an all-terrain vehicle. The gun had a range of 1.25–2.5 miles and a yield of 10–20 tons of TNT. This image was classified when it was made and was not declassified until after the weapon went out of service in 1971.

Beginning in 1982, Project REARM upgraded the arsenal to a modern, world-class manufacturing facility. A new complex was added to the buildings from the 1920s and 1940s. In this photograph from December 1987, the new REARM construction is on the right. On the left is World War II's massive Building 208. After REARM was completed in 1988, production was moved from the last shop, and Rodman's era was officially over.

This last image is from the Rock Island Arsenal centennial celebration and captures old and new around 1962. On the left is a replica of Fort Armstrong erected on its centennial in 1916. To the right is an M31 Honest John rocket and launcher fielded in 1954. The Rock Island Arsenal developed the truck-mounted launch structure.

DISCOVER THOUSANDS OF LOCAL HISTORY BOOKS
FEATURING MILLIONS OF VINTAGE IMAGES

Arcadia Publishing, the leading local history publisher in the United States, is committed to making history accessible and meaningful through publishing books that celebrate and preserve the heritage of America's people and places.

Find more books like this at
www.arcadiapublishing.com

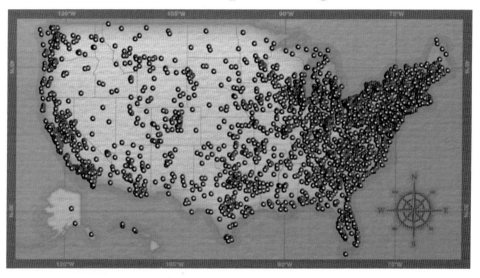

Search for your hometown history, your old stomping grounds, and even your favorite sports team.